Sheep on the Farm

by Mari C. Schuh

Consulting Editor: Gail Saunders-Smith, Ph.D.

Consultant: Mike Caskey
Former President, National Sheep Association
Instructor, Lamb and Wool Program
Minnesota West Community and Technical College

Pebble Books

an imprint of Capstone Press
Mankato, Minnesota

Pebble Books are published by Capstone Press
151 Good Counsel Drive, P.O. Box 669, Mankato, Minnesota 56002
http://www.capstone-press.com

1 2 3 4 5 6 07 06 05 04 03 02

Library of Congress Cataloging-in-Publication Data
Schuh, Mari C., 1975–
     Sheep on the farm / by Mari C. Schuh.
     p. cm.—(On the farm)
     Includes bibliographical references (p. 23) and index.
     ISBN 0-7368-0994-5
     1. Sheep—Juvenile literature. [1. Sheep.] I. Title. II. Series.
SF375.2 .S38 2002
636.3—dc21   2001000464

JE
SCH
C.1

Summary: Simple text and photographs present sheep and how they are raised.

Note to Parents and Teachers

The On the Farm series supports national science standards related
to life science. This book describes and illustrates sheep on the
farm. The photographs support early readers in understanding the
text. The repetition of words and phrases helps early readers learn
new words. This book also introduces early readers to subject-
specific vocabulary words, which are defined in the Words to Know
section. Early readers may need assistance to read some words and
to use the Table of Contents, Words to Know, Read More, Internet
Sites, and Index/Word List sections of the book.

Table of Contents

wool

ears

legs

legs

4

Sheep live on farms
and ranches.

Sheep live in groups called flocks.

Most sheep live outdoors.

Sheep graze on grass and other plants.

Farmers feed hay
and grain to sheep.

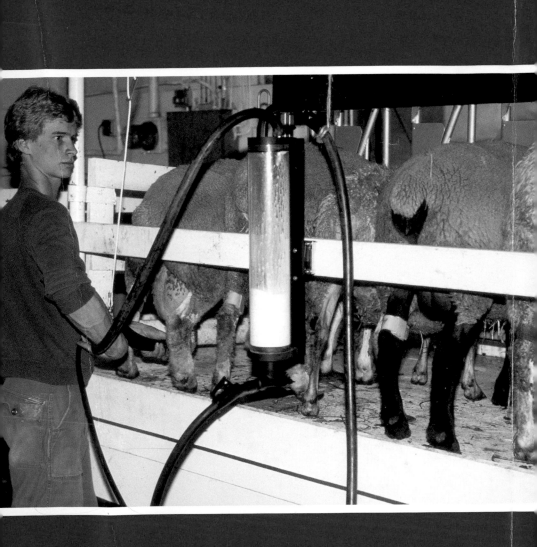

Farmers raise sheep
for their meat, wool,
and milk. Farmers use
machines to milk sheep.

Farmers shear wool off sheep.

ram

ewe

18

A male sheep is called a ram. A female sheep is called a ewe.

Sheep bleat.

Words to Know

bleat—the noise a sheep makes

flock—a group of animals of one kind that live, travel, or eat together; sheep live in flocks; some flocks have as many as 3,000 sheep.

graze—to eat grass and other plants that are growing in a field; sheep eat fresh grass, hay, and grain.

meat—the flesh of an animal that can be eaten; the meat of a sheep is called lamb or mutton.

raise—to care for animals as they grow and become older

shear—to cut off the wool of a sheep; farmers shear sheep with electric clippers; shearing does not hurt sheep.

wool—the soft, thick, curly hair of sheep; wool is used to make yarn and fabric.

Read More

Bell, Rachael. *Sheep.* Farm Animals. Chicago: Heinemann Library, 2000.

Miller, Sara Swan. *Sheep.* A True Book. New York: Children's Press, 2000.

Stone, Lynn M. *Sheep Have Lambs.* Animals and Their Young. Minneapolis: Compass Point Books, 2000.

Internet Sites

All about Sheep for Kids
http://www.kiddyhouse.com/Farm/Sheep

Learning about Sheep
http://www.sheepusa.org/fkids.htm

Kids Farm: Sheep
http://www.kidsfarm.com/sheep.htm

Sheep Printout
http://www.ZoomDinosaurs.com/subjects/mammals/farm/Sheepprintout.shtml

Index/Word List

Word Count: 66
Early-Intervention Level: 9

Credits

Heather Kindseth, cover designer; Heidi Meyer, production designer; Kimberly Danger and Deirdre Barton, photo researchers

David F. Clobes, Stock Photography, 12
Frank Siteman/Pictor, 16
International Stock/Tom & Michele Grimm, 6
Paul Dalzell/Pictor, cover
Photri-Microstock, 18 (bottom)
Pictor, 10
University of Minnesota, 14
Visuals Unlimited/Beth Davidow, 1; William J. Webber, 4; Rob & Ann Simpson, 8; Corinne Humphrey, 18 (top); Janine Pestel, 20